WINGS No.

Red Star Fighters
& Ground Attack

Hans Halberstadt

Windrow & Greene

©1994 Windrow & Greene Ltd.
Published in Great Britain 1994 by
Windrow & Greene Ltd.
5 Gerrard Street
London W1V 7LJ

A CIP catalogue record for this
book is available from the
British Library.

ISBN 1-872004-83-0

Published in the USA by
Specialty Press Publishers
   & Wholesalers Inc.
11481 Kost Dam Road
North Branch, MN 55056
(612) 583 3471/ fax 583 2023

**(Title page) The commander of
the MiG-29 squadron at Kubinka,
Col.Alexander Kutuzov, begins
the engine start sequence in a
UB trainer version of the
Fulcrum, which lacks radar.**

**(Front cover) Maj.Alexander
Datalov, Russian Air Force,
poses on his Sukhoi Su-27
Flanker. The big red Soviet star
on the fin has survived the
bewildering changes of recent
years; this emblem remains one
of the few stable elements in the
life of today's Russian pilots.**

The Curtain Lifts

The big, rugged Sukhoi Su-24 *Fencer* multi-role bomber, whose design and mission are comparable to those of the F-111, is just one of the combat types based at Kubinka near Moscow. This machine waits on the flight line between training missions.

Back in the long, frozen decades of the Cold War confrontation between the forces of the Warsaw Pact and NATO, you heard basically two things about Russian combat equipment: it was either as crude and simple as a club, or it was extremely sophisticated and dangerous. This contradiction made it very difficult to think or talk clearly about Soviet weapons of any sort – and particularly about combat aircraft, those fuzzy shapes that occasionally appeared in specialist magazines, or the US Department of Defense's annual publication *Soviet Military Power.*

Then came Gorbachev, *perestroika,* and the stunningly rapid collapse of the whole Soviet system. Beginning with the appearance of the MiG-29 *Fulcrum* at England's 1988 Farnborough Air Show, the NATO nations finally got a good look at the aircraft they had been training to fight for so long. The revelation was shocking.

The MiG-29 flew manoeuvers that simply could not be duplicated by Western combat aircraft. It had features that enhanced the tactical performance of the aircraft in ways that equivalent NATO fighters could not match. The Russians, accused for years of building crude "boilermaker's" copies of NATO technologies, demonstrated that they were innovative, imaginative, highly creative designers; suddenly they were getting credit for blazing trails into places that European and American designers had not explored.

Of course, none of this actually proved that the MiG was the best lightweight contender for the Air Combat Championship of the World – because the only real way to do that is to have a war and see what happens. But there was a kind of war at Farnborough 1988; and, although the French (predictably) cried "foul", all the judges agreed that the Russians won the public relations contest by a knockout. It was not just the features of the airplanes, or the flight manoeuvers, or even the tremendous personal charm of the representatives from Mikoyan; it was *everything*, together, and it was dazzling.

The next year, 1989, the Russians brought the bigger Su-27 *Flanker* to the Paris Air Show. Again, the Soviet aircraft astounded NATO observers with flight manoeuvers, design details, and tactical potential that were far more advanced than anything anticipated. Even the ejection seat fitted to the MiG-29 and Su-27 was dramatically demonstrated to be at least as good as anything in Western combat aircraft when a low-level bird strike forced Anatoly Kvotcher to punch out of his *Fulcrum* in front of the crowd – in a nearly impossible flight attitude – to a safe landing. Even Lockheed's *Air Power* newsletter proclaimed, "... the MiG-29 and Su-27 are sportier than anything we have in the inventory."

Since those first revelations just a few years ago the Russians have gleefully exhibited their aviation technology to the world, and have rapidly received

(Left) Numerous post-war Russian aircraft, missiles, tanks and artillery can be found – alongside the excellent displays commemorating the Soviet victory in the Great Patriotic War – at the Red Army Museum, Moscow; it's a little off the beaten track, but well worth the effort of a visit.

(Right) An early *Flanker*, out to pasture, is one of many combat aircraft on static display on the site of the old Moscow municipal airport; the visitor will find this only about three miles from the Kremlin, a few minutes' ride out of town on the Green Line.

the respect and admiration of the aerospace community for their many great accomplishments. A number of foreign journalists have been invited to visit the design bureaux, research facilities, and air force bases; and I have been privileged to be among them.

My first visit was in 1991, and it was full of surprises. After many years of working with the US Army, Navy, Marine Corps and Air Force – and a fair amount of study and preparation for the trip – I thought I had a pretty good idea of what to expect; but nearly everything I had heard was wrong. The people were generally charming and friendly, the food was wonderful, and the access to aircraft and flight crews was even better than my experience with the US Air Force. I was allowed into the cockpits of MiG-29s, -25s and -31s, Sukhoi Su-24s, -25s, and -27s, to document military technologies that were state secrets only months previously. I was invited to fly in both the *Flanker* and the *Fulcrum* (and told by Major Alexander Datalov, one of the Sukhoi pilots, that they too used the NATO name for the aircraft, although he wished it had a good Russian name!)

Russia is a fascinating country to visit for many reasons, despite what you've been told. Besides the fine arts museums and conventional cultural attractions, Moscow has some of the most interesting military and aviation museums anywhere. Just a couple of miles from the Kremlin, right up the Leningradski Prospekt, is the site of Moscow's old airport; if you hop on the Metro and get off at the Airport stop, you can walk over to an open-air museum dedicated to modern Russian military aircraft. For the equivalent of a few pennies you are allowed to wander among the MiG-29s, Su-27s, MiG-27s, and even an early Mi-24 *Hind*. Actually, all the aircraft seem to be pretty early models, and all are fighters or ground attack planes – there isn't enough room for *Bears* or *Blackjacks*. This certainly isn't the only museum in Moscow where you can examine Russian fighter aircraft, it just happens to be the one dedicated to this particular art form.

One aviation museum you might have trouble visiting is inside the guarded confines of the Moscow Aviation Institute, along the Leningradski Prospekt in what I call the "Russian aviation ghetto". Here, cheek-by-jowl, are almost all the design bureaux, huge buildings full of designers and plans and ideas; and nearly all of the thousands of designers are graduates of the Moscow Aviation Institute up the street. I got a tour of the institute and a look at its extensive collection of engines, airframes and landing gear. During the tour I noticed one component that had a familiar look to it; closer inspection revealed that it was the stripped-down ejection capsule from an F-111, complete with bullet hole on the left side – a donation from the North Vietnamese, and a reminder that the friendly relations between our communities are a very new and exotic development.

Kubinka

Drive out of Moscow on the Minsk highway for about an hour and a half and you will arrive at the small town of Kubinka. Turn off the highway down a country road, through the pretty little village of Respeche, and you will arrive at the gate to the old Russian Air Force base known as Kubinka. The base dates all the way back to 1930, and launched thousands of missions against the Nazis during the terrible years we call World War II and the Russians call

the Great Patriotic War. Kubinka was never actually captured by the Germans, although the high-water mark of the Panzers' advance lapped against the northern suburbs of Moscow.

Kubinka has occasionally been referred to as a "show base" by Western observers; but apart from a small demonstration area it is a working facility not very different from its Western counterparts – and not very showy at all. The combat aircraft are parked in dispersal areas, behind berms and patrolled by guards. Some are stored in reinforced concrete shelters. Missiles, rockets, cannon ammunition and bombs are stored in the ordnance shelters. Out on the flight line, over in the parking and maintenance areas, the crews service, arm, maintain, launch, and recover the MiG-29s, Su-25s, *Flankers* and *Fencers* that call Kubinka home. There is nothing ornamental or elegant about any of it; the great majority of Kubinka is a place where people and airplanes prepare for war.

Most of the residents are, unlike those of American or British bases, officers; there are very few enlisted soldiers on the base, and the few present are engaged in the least skilled occupations. I didn't know that at first, with embarrassing results: I assumed that the young mechanic/crew chief I met was (like his USAF counterparts) a sergeant. Instead he turned out to be a lieutenant, intent on making his career in the Russian Air Force. It seems to be a

good system; the professionalism of these critical personnel is assured. They have status, continuity, and extensive training – unlike the conscript soldiers who assist with the heavy lifting.

Kubinka isn't fancy, but it is certainly a desirable posting. That's because it is close to Moscow, and the train station is a short walk from the main gate. Officers and their families are housed – like almost everybody else – in apartment buildings that provide basic, somewhat cramped, accommodations. But nearly every officer has his own private little country *dacha* down the road for weekends and vacations. The government housing may be stark, efficient concrete, but the *dachas* are often beautiful examples of traditional, elegant Russian carpentry.

I visited one of the pilots, Valery Kravtsov, a very young lieutenant-colonel who commanded the Su-25 *Frogfoot* squadron. We sat in the kitchen while he served tea and a light snack – which in Russia normally means about 3,000 calories worth of cakes, candy, cookies, bread and butter. A visit to a Russian pilot's apartment is like a visit to just about any military pilot's government-furnished housing anywhere: the quarters are a bit cramped, but adequate. Valery likes to build model aircraft and has a display of them in the living room, very much like those in the quarters of my friends who fly F-111s from Cannon Air Force Base, New Mexico.

Kubinka feels more like a park than an airbase –

(Left) Russian ground crews endure the same kind of duty parades as in any other army, with the added discomfort of extreme cold. Their winter clothing – like much of the flight gear issued to aircrew – is well made, suited to the conditions, and very comfortable. On the flagpole the old Russian tricolour has now replaced the red banner. *(SergeySkrynnikov/AviaData via Arms Communications)*

The enlisted personnel at Kubinka are mostly limited to menial duties. The appearance of this gate guard, and the roadway repair detail, suggests the survival (so far) of the old Soviet practice of giving more than their share of such work to conscripts from the eastern and southern republics, often many thousands of miles and several time-zones from their homes.

Random portraits of Air Force officers. Nearly all the personnel at Kubinka are commissioned ranks, and many do jobs that would fall to sergeants in the Western forces. (This, and the rarity of saluting by enlisted men, led the author into some embarrassment.) The system makes sense – the crew chiefs are professionals, part of the team for the long haul, with responsibility and authority. Despite what we have been told for decades about the low motivation of Soviet weapons maintenance crews, as far as the author could see they are the same sort of hard-charging, well-trained team players as you would find on the flight lines at Nellis or Luke. Note that the old Soviet star, hammer and sickle insignia still adorn the Air Force's blue-piped caps – though for how long is anybody's guess.

except when a flight of *Flankers* is taking off, or when a *Frogfoot* pilot gets playful over the runway before entering the pattern. The streets are heavily tree-lined, and the forest is deep around the hangars and bunkers. Officers and their wives stroll the grounds arm in arm; the enlisted soldiers they pass never seem to salute. Down in the operations building, next to the flight line, the pilots stow their gear and get their briefings. They also take lunch in the pilots' dining room, served by perky waitresses instead of going through serving lines as American pilots normally do. Aircraft service records are kept here, maintained by several eye-catching ladies who turn out to be pilots' wives.

Russian Design Tradition

Until recently, Russian design bureaux were – like everything else – government-owned and operated. But even so, they were much more like private companies in the Western tradition, strongly influenced by the leadership, vision, and political talent of the men who founded and directed them, and who gave their names to them – men like Mikoyan, Sukhoi, Antonov, Ilyushin, and many others well known to Russians.

Right up until the demise of the Soviet Union it was conventional wisdom in the West that Soviet aircraft were rude, crude designs, shamelessly copied from Western technologies that were, as often as not, stolen by spies. Well, the Russians read these reports along with the rest of us, and it's kind of fun to watch them when they try to talk about the issue of pirated technology, copied designs, and just who is copying whom – because they tend to splutter, fume, and turn bright colors all at once!

From their point of view – supported by their documentation – it has been Western designers who have been copying Russian innovations. They point out that they used "fly-by-wire" controls first, and pioneered and innovated many developments well before Lockheed or McDonnell Douglas got around to copying Mikoyan or Sukhoi. My friend Alexander ("Sasha") Velovitch, who worked for many years as a Western technology assessment specialist for Mikoyan, says "...It has always been interesting to read in Western publications that the *Fulcrum's* radar was based on stolen APG-65 technology. I wish that were true! Why is it that nobody believes the Westinghouse APQ-164 phased array radar on the Rockwell B-1B bomber was copied from the MiG-31's radar – the first of its type, introduced years earlier than the APQ-164?"

(Right) The high proportion of career officers stationed at Kubinka means that it is a family-oriented installation. This lady, the wife of one of the Air Force officers, has a job of her own on the base. Typical of many of the women you meet in Russian cities today, she's well-educated, well-informed, stylish – and apprehensive about the many changes forced upon her family over the past couple of years.

(Left) Mikhail Waldenberg, the chief designer of the MiG-29, and a charming, genial spokesman for the Mikoyan OKB. Waldenberg has worked on the MiG-15, -17, -19, -21 and -25, and is an enthusiastic advocate for Russian design traditions and achievements.

(Below) In its day the MiG-21 was a world class interceptor, fighter- bomber and recce aircraft, with J-band interception radar, slightly better than Mach 2 maximum speed from a Turmansky R-13- 300 turbojet producing about 15,000 pounds of thrust in burner, and a range of about 690 miles on internal fuel. The *Fishbed*, as NATO gracelessly dubbed it, carried a wide variety of weapons on four underwing pylons: rockets of several sizes, IR missiles, cannon (in a pack under the fuselage), or camera packs, electronic warfare sensors and jammers.

(Above) The braking parachute being stowed in its container in the tail of a MiG-21. *(Sergey Skrynnikov/AviaData via Arms/ Communications)*

(Below) The Sukhoi Su-15 received the NATO codename *Flagon* when it first flew in about 1967. In those days it was the pride of the Frontal Aviation interceptor squadrons, a Mach 2.1 single-seater mounting two 23mm cannon and racks for *Aphid* or *Anab* missiles.

An old Su-15 from the air defense regiment at Kromatorsk in the Ukraine is readied for a training sortie. *(Sergey Skrynnikov/AviaData via Arms Communications)*

(Left and Right) The Sukhoi Su-17 *Fitter* first flew in the mid-1960s, and the basic airframe was produced under three designations. The Su-17 was a popular ground attack and close support aircraft with a wide variety of applications; it mounted a 30mm cannon in each wingroot, and eight weapons pylons under the wings and fuselage. (The Su-20 and Su-22 were somewhat less capable export versions.) The intake accomodates an SRD-5M radar, codenamed *High Fix* by NATO: a rangefinding system integrated into the fire control computer. This K-model includes laser rangefinder (small window), Doppler radar, and head-up display.

(Right) This handsome MiG-23 *Flogger's* flying days are over, though it still draws an admiring crowd of museum visitors. Many others are still in squadron service, however, with the air forces of several nations. This swing-wing design was first delivered in 1973; it is a single-seater fighter-bomber with a 23mm cannon, five weapons pylons, and a combat radius of over 800 miles.

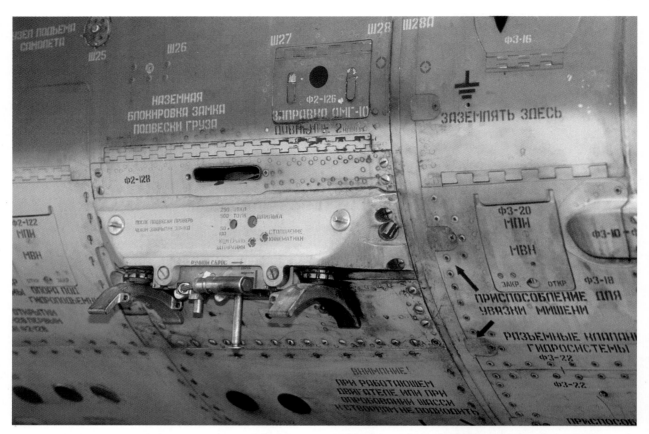

Close-ups of the articulated main landing gear assembly, wheel well, and one of the fuselage weapons stations of the MiG-27 *Flogger,* a development of the MiG-23.

MiG-25 "Foxbat"

(Above) The crew chief, a lieutenant, unlatches the canopy of a *Foxbat* prior to flight operations.

(Right) The MiG trademark is visible on most of the products of the Mikoyan bureau.

(Previous page) The MiG-25's development helped to change NATO tactics; this Mach 3-plus interceptor was one of the reasons high altitude penetration missions were abandoned in favour of an under-the- radar approach. When that change had been completed the MiG-25 was suddenly obsolete; but it still serves – and it was the foundation for the MiG-31, the low-level interceptor with a slightly lower speed but a much better low altitude performance.

(Right) MiG-25 nosewheel. The mudguard has an important function, keeping gravel, rocks and loose bits of runway from being kicked back into the engine intakes. The Russians operate from far less pristine surfaces than most Western aircrews demand, and their equipment is designed accordingly.

A rare look deep inside the cavernous air intake of a MiG-25 *Foxbat.*

(Right) While you're standing on the port intake just before slithering into the MiG-25 cockpit, take a look aft at that immense airfoil – most of it made of nickel steel, too. This aircraft may be the apogee of the straight-ahead, balls-to-the-wall interceptor, a Mach 3 airplane that now has to live in a Mach 2 world.

(Right, below) Even the big MiG-25 is designed to be able to tolerate rough expeditionary airfields little better than the sort that the US Marines carve out for their Harriers. The Moscow Aviation Institute accordingly maintains a large collection of exotic landing gear designs – most even kinkier than this example.

(Below) The *Foxbat's* starboard side inboard weapons pylon, with the ECM fairing visible low in the left background. MiG-25 construction includes a lot of nickel steel alloy rather than aluminium (but the rumour about the crews having to oil the skin to keep it from rusting isn't true).

MiG-29 "Fulcrum"

The world-famous Mikoyan OKB dates back to World War II and a friendship between two extremely gifted young aircraft designers, Anusahvan ("Artyom") Mikoyan and Mikhail Gurevich. Their partnership produced some of the most famous and innovative aircraft of the post-war period: the MiG-15, a squirming, agile jet fighter that came as a highly unpleasant surprise to US and Allied fighter pilots in the Korean War; the MiG-25, with its Mach 3-plus speed; and the amazing MiG-29, an airplane that has dazzled military observers and air show audiences since its first appearance in the West in 1988.

The MiG-29 is the airplane that started the "attitude adjustment" among Western observers with its appearance at that unforgettable Farnborough Air Show. The MiG's agility – its ability to sustain controlled flight at extreme angles of attack and at very low speeds, its rates of acceleration and decelera-

tion – was superior to any NATO combat aircraft. (That certainly does not mean that it is the best fighter – just the most agile.)

The MiG-29 is a "counter-air" fighter, a dog-fighter, that can also be used for ground attack missions. It is currently in the service of many nations, including India, Iraq, Iran, Libya, North Korea, Germany (and possibly the US Air Force, as a participant in the dissimilar air combat training program based at Nellis AFB, Nevada). It is currently being withdrawn from Russian service in favor of the bigger Su-27, despite howls of protest from many senior Russian Air Force generals.

The MiG-29 is a lightweight modern Mach 2-plus air-to-air fighter with a secondary role as an interceptor; it has a maximum range of about 1,300 miles, and a maximum take-off weight of about 40,000 pounds – though not both at the same time. Its service ceiling is around 56,000 feet; light and

MiG-29UB *Fulcrum* of the Swifts aerobatic team on very, very short final, about half a second from touchdown. The landing attitude is critical on the MiG-29, with little clearance for the tail cone, so landing speeds tend to be rather hot – even when the braking parachute is deployed (as it often is, with a loud pop) at about this point.

clean, the *Fulcrum* will go upstairs at the rate of about 65,000 feet per minute, which means that the controls will go mushy and the nose will pitch over about 50 seconds after take-off – a short trip to inner space.

Up at flight level 350 or so, where the engines are designed to function best, the MiG-29 will perk along at Mach 2.3 or better, with the burner lit. You don't do that for long before the tanks go dry, but the speed would have been useful for intercepting any pesky Strike Eagles or AWACS planes intruding on Mother Russia's airspace.

The MiG-29 was developed by Mikoyan OKB as an internal project, much as European or American companies routinely develop concepts for future models independently of government intervention or funding. The *Fulcrum* became a glimmer in somebody's eye back in the 1960s in response to radical changes in NATO air battle tactics. Until then, Soviet and Warsaw Pact expectations were of an encounter with NATO forces that would feature high-altitude engagements – a battle the Soviets were perfectly prepared to win with their excellent surface-to-air missiles, radar net, and interceptor force. NATO countered those defenses with low level tactics and aircraft able to sweep in under the radar net, below the SAMs' effective engagement limits, and down among the radar clutter where the MiG-25s and Sukhois of the 1960s couldn't see them. The F-111 Aardvark (see the present author's title Wings 4 in this series) was just one of the responses.

The *Fulcrum* was designed around its look-down, shoot-down radar, coupled to BVR air-to-air missiles and a reasonably fast, extremely manoeu-vrable airframe. According to Mikhail Waldenberg, the aircraft's chief designer, the design came togeth-er in 1972; the prototype first flew in 1977, and *Fulcrum* entered service in 1982.

The MiG-29 airframe features extensive composites and advanced alloys to keep the weight of the aircraft down. The fuselage is blended, with a smooth, lift-generating airfoil shape reminiscent of the F-16 Falcon. The cockpit is placed well forward of the wing for visibility. Wingspan is a little over 37 feet, with an area of about 379 square feet.

One of the great satisfactions for Waldenberg and the rest of the design team seems to be the performance of the integrated weapons package, particularly the way the 30mm cannon is integrated with the fire control system. They claim a guaranteed kill with the cannon with the first five-round burst. That may have more to do with the precision of the laser rangefinder than the cannon itself, but the distinction is academic if you are on the receiving end. Only 150 of the huge, two-pound shells are carried, but according to Waldenberg that is enough for 30 enemy aircraft – more than enough for most missions, he seems to think.

Both the MiG-29 and the Su-27 employ a system that added to the fascination when these airplanes were first displayed: a passive infrared tracker that offers some of the advantages of radar without the tell-tale radiation. The system is known in the West as IRST – Infra Red Seek and Track. Within about ten miles, the IRST will track a target (tail-on, in military power – the range is much greater if the target is in afterburner) and provide data to the fire control computer to engage.

The radar, an integral part of the weapons system, can be configured to provide a back-up to the IRST, and will only transmit when the target's IR signature will not permit the passive thermal sensor to lock on – as, for example, when the target gets out of the system's range, or in cloud or rain. Once the IRST regains contact the radar stops transmitting, and the target loses the MiG from his radar attack warning (RAW) scope. According to my spies at

(Left) Although new to the air show circuit the Russians work hard at coming up with dramatic routines, and they fly a tight, precise six-ship show. At Kubinka the show aircraft mingle freely with the tactical aircraft on the flight line.

(Right) This underside view of a MiG-29 shows a pair of red-painted AA- 10d *Alamo* extended-range IR-guided missiles, and four short-range IR-guided AA-11 *Archers*; the black bands indicate practice rounds. *(Sergey Skrynnikov/AirData via Arms Communications)*

(Below) Col.Alexander Kutuzov, deputy commander of the Kubinka air regiment (equivalent to a Western air wing) and leader of the MiG-29 demonstration team, the Swifts.

Mikoyan (actually, chief test pilot Anatoly Kvotcher), the N-019E radar works equally well against "look-down" targets as against those above the aircraft. Detection range is about 50 miles head on, about 30 miles in tail chase.

External stores are carried on six pylons: 80mm rockets, heat-seeking dog-fight missiles, and BVR radar-guided missiles can all be employed, besides the 30mm cannon installed in the right wing root fairing. The MiG-29 can attack ground targets, but only in daylight and in visual contact. The *Fulcrum's* weapons delivery system includes a pilot's helmet sight similar to the one found on the US Army's AH-64 Apache attack helicopter. This permits the pilot to designate a target while in "HOTAS" mode, steering the missile seeker heads, the IRST and the radar to "look" in the direction the pilot indicates.

The MiG-29's powerplant is a pair of widely spaced Isotov RD-33 turbofans, each generating 18,300 pounds of thrust in afterburner. They seem to be extremely stable powerplants, tolerant of extreme operating conditions. The engines have a novel and complex intake system, with primary and secondary inlets to permit the aircraft to operate from rough fields where foreign object damage would otherwise be a problem. The primary intake doors are normally closed when the landing gear is lowered; inlet air is then furnished by louvres on the upper side of the wing leading edge extensions, just aft of the cockpit. While it appears that this would severely limit intake air volume and make the probablity of an engine stall much more likely, the engines keep running even during the tail-slide manoeuver that was one of the first surprises for the crowd at Farnborough in 1988. The ability of this engine to maintain a healthy flow of air even when the whole airplane is sliding backward through (very low altitude) airspace is just about unique, and is a testament to both the engine and the intake design.

Unfortunately, these doors were wide open when Anatoly Kvotcher made his low-level tail-slide at Paris in 1989. As he came out of minimum power to full afterburner, after hovering in space for a moment, one of the engines sucked up a small flock of seagulls; one or two would not normally be a

Col.Kutuzov wearing the new lightweight flying helmet, and the fleece-collared dark blue winter flight uniform worn over G-suits in cold weather. Russian flight equipment turns out to be well made and comfortable – the oxygen mask, in particular, is much pleasanter to wear than the US type.

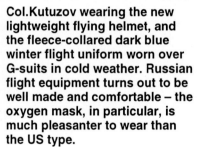

Col.Kutuzov on the "hold short" line, waiting for his clearance from the tower to take the active.

(Left) MiG-29 in your face... The glass sphere is the "eye" of the amazing IRST (infrared seek and track) system and the laser rangefinder.

(Right) MiG-29 fin construction features extensive use of composites, and they are embellished with many aerials and antennae; the fairing above the rudder is the rearward-pointing electronic warning antenna which searches for the signals from enemy fighters' radar.

Most of Kubinka's MiG-29 fleet are warriors, not showmen, and are housed accordingly. This aircraft, tucked into its woodland revetment, will have instruments and controls in its cockpit which are removed from the *Fulcrums* that visit overseas airshows.

(Above) MiG-29 underside, with air intake doors open for inspection.

(Left, above) RD-33 inlet and first compressor stage. Maj. Bob Wade, the Canadian F-18 jockey who was the first NATO combat pilot to fly the MiG-29, judges the RD-33 a good, reliable engine by Western standards, and very powerful in afterburner.

(Left) Detail of the accessory section of the RD-33 engine.

problem, and even this bunch would not have been indigestible if Kvotcher had had a few thousand feet of airspace to recover; but the affected engine flamed out while the other was at full thrust. The differential thrust rolled the MiG over on its back, out of control, in front of thousands of people. Kvotcher punched out at the last possible millisecond, and the MiG augered in – to the malicious satisfaction of many sales staff from the other manufacturers present.

There are currently four versions of the MiG-29. The standard single-seat A-model is in widespread service. The two-seat trainer UB-model has a periscope viewer for the rear seat crew member; lacking radar, the MiG-29UB is not – unlike the UB version of the *Flanker* – an operational combat aircraft but is used solely for training. The newer C-model, first delivered in 1989, has a more pronounced hump behind the cockpit for additional internal fuel and avionics. Finally the K-model, a navalized version, lacks the FOD intake doors, but has a beefed-up landing gear, in-flight refueling capability, folding wings, and an arrestor hook.

MiG-31 "Foxhound"

A MiG-31 *Foxhound A* slides
down the runway at Zhukovskiy
Flight Research Institute with
Mikoyan's famous test pilot
Valery Menitsky at the controls.
*(Sergey Skrynnikov/AviaData via
Arms Communications)*

Head-on view of the MiG-31 with the back-seater's periscope extended.

(Right) Detail views of the front cockpit of the MiG-31 *Foxhound*, almost identical to that of the MiG-25.

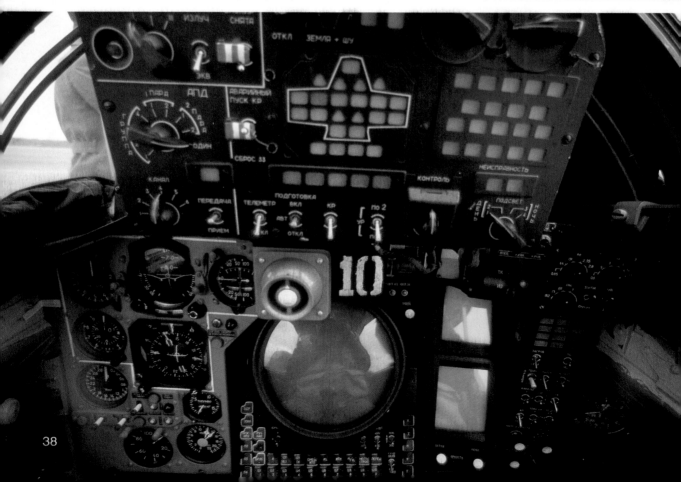

(Left) A very few years ago these photos would have been worth a fortune – or maybe the author's life – and they are still a rarity: they show the aft cockpit of the dreaded MiG-31. This weapons systems officer's station represents the apogee of Russian manned interceptor design and technology, and is the place where the Soviet Union expected to begin to defeat the low-level deep penetration attack which NATO forces would have executed in the event of war. Although provided with basic flight controls and instrumentation, the WSO is supposed to keep his nose glued to the *Foxhound's* superior radar and IRST. The man who occupies this seat operates Russia's most capable long-range interceptor weapons system, with the ability to detect targets at 185 miles, track at 168, and engage multiple bogies simultaneously.

(Above) MiG-31 pitot tube detail.

(Below) ECM pod on the underside of the MiG-31 *Foxhound.*

Su-24 "Fencer"

Kubinka owns and operates a squadron of *Fencers*, and during my visit I had a chance to see many of them launched and recovered from training missions, to clamber into the left seat, and to explore this fascinating aircraft's anatomy in intimate detail. The *Fencer* crews are a very intense and business-like lot; no sooner are they on the ground than they start enthusiastically debriefing with their mates – before they even get their helmets off.

The Sukhoi Su-24 is a multi-role aircraft, able to execute strategic bombing, attack, reconnaissance and interdiction missions. That means that it can go low or high, fast or slow, bomb from any flight attitude, and deliver a wide variety of ordnance to support the ground commander in the field. It is, in many respects, similar to the F-111 Aardvark, NATO's version of the same swing-wing attack/interdiction/strategic concept.

The Su-24 *Fencer C* is a Mach 2-plus attack bomber with a maximum take-off weight of about 87,000 pounds; about 24,000 pounds of that can be weapons load. Combat radius with that load and internal fuel for a low-level mission will be about 200 miles, but with lighter loads and a "high-low-high" mission profile the combat radius can be stretched to over 800 miles; with in-flight refueling *(Fencer D* and *E)* that can stretch to the crew endurance limits. Service ceiling is about 57,000 feet. Published maximum speed (clean) is Mach 2.18 at altitude; estimated low-level maximum penetration speed is about Mach 1.2.

The first production models of the *Fencer* were delivered in 1974, well after the F-111 Aardvark. While the *Fencer* might have been inspired by the American low-level attack/strike bomber, it was also heavily influenced by a British design, the TSR-2. Both were intended to be high speed, low level, deep penetration bombers; but the fixed-wing TSR-2 was aborted by a British Labour government on cost grounds in 1965. Sukhoi's first prototype was also a fixed-wing design; but the swing wing, with all its

When a flight of two Sukhoi Su-24M *Fencers* leave the nest the ground rumbles as the big Lyulka ALF-21F-3 turbojets blast out 50,000 pounds of thrust in afterburner. Note the full-span flaps. About 800 *Fencers* have been manufactured since the type first appeared in the mid-1970s, and serve with the Russian and several other air forces; this successful design is likely to be a player for several years to come.

weight and complexity, was finally included in the design, and the first production models started displacing the old Yak-28 *Brewers* in 1974.

The *Fencer* is a large aircraft, 69 feet long and 57 feet from tip to tip, wings spread. Construction is of the conventional semi-monocoque design common to most military aircraft of this vintage. The undercarriage elements are all mounted in the fuselage portion of the airframe, with dual wheels on the main and nose gear. The *Fencer* is quite capable of operating out of rough improvised airfields or dirt roads if required, and the landing gear and other elements of the airframe were designed with that in mind. The air intakes, well aft of the cockpit, have variable intake ramps. The fin is a large single unit with a housing for the braking parachute stowed directly over the nozzles; huge stabilators provide tremendous roll or pitch authority.

Like the Aardvark, the Su-24 uses a variable-geometry wing; sweep angle stops are 16, 45 and about 60 degrees. The weapons pylons on the outboard section of the wing pivot to keep the stores aligned with the aircraft centreline – just one of the tricky engineering problems that beset design teams who want to build innovative aircraft. With the wings retracted for high-speed flight, the span is reduced to only 33 feet. Extended, the wings provide about 450 square feet of airfoil area. The wing is equipped with leading edge slats across the full span, plus large two-section flaps on the outer wing trailing edges. The wing also includes integral spoilers just ahead of the flaps for low-speed manoeuvers and for landing.

The cockpit is a side-by-side arrangement, rather spacious by comparison with the single-seat pits of the MiG and Sukhoi fighters. The *Fencer* has two

In USAF terms, this Su-24 is performing a "combat turn": as soon as it lands from a sortie it is quickly refueled and rearmed to bring it back to combat readiness.

radar systems: a terrain-following radar for navigation, and an attack radar for precision delivery of weapons in any weather, day or night. And the weapons system officer ("*shturman*") seems to have a very precise delivery system: according to US Army Lt.Gen. Donald Keith, who studied the aircraft in detail, the Su-24 "...has the capability to deliver ordnance in all weather to within 55 metres (180 feet) of its target."

The *Fencer* has two weapons stations on the outboard wing section, four on the fuselage, and two on the wing root. The fuselage pylons have more ground clearance than the F-111 wing offers, allowing installation of bulky weapons on all the stations, not just the ones on the wing. The *Fencers* operating out of Kubinka while I was there were busy expending ordnance as fast as the ground crews could refuel and rearm the aircraft with 30mm cannon ammunition, rockets and small practice bombs. In the US Air Force this recycling is called a "combat turn", and its speed and efficiency is an essential element in the combat effectiveness of a unit. The Russians execute their combat turns with really amazing dispatch.

The Su-24 will deliver just about anything that will fit on the pylons, from unguided free-flight rockets to nuclear bombs to precision missiles of the AS-7, -10, and -14 type. A multi-barrel 30mm rotary cannon is housed on the right side of the fuselage to provide industrial-strength direct fire to ground targets – and perhaps the odd airborne encounter, if things get really close. While hosing ground targets is not exactly this aircraft's forte, it is supposed to be a ground attack platform, and accurate cannon fire is still one of the fundamental tricks of the trade.

The low-level/high-speed mission of the deep

(Right) A partial load of 80mm free-flight rockets about to be loaded into one of the launch canisters of a *Fencer*.

penetration bomber is a challenge to aircraft engine designers. Fuel economy is, of necessity, awful. Even so, *Fencer* seems to have the highest thrust-to-weight ratio in its class – better than the Tornado or the Aardvark – thanks to its twin Lyulka AL-21F-3 turbojets. Each of these engines puts out up to 25,000 pounds of thrust in afterburner (although not for long before the tanks go dry). This engine is a derivative of the tried and true powerplant installed on the Su-17. About 2,900 (Imp.) gallons of fuel are carried internally, with provision for four external tanks plumbed to the pylons.

The C-model *Fencer* is the most common, introduced in 1981, but a Delta version went into service two years later, offering in-flight refueling. You can spot the D (Su-24M) most readily by its longer nose and big wing fences. The D is also available in a recce version, employed by both the Air Force and Navy. A dedicated electronic warfare version, NATO designation *Fencer E,* is assigned the same kind of missions as the EF-111A Raven – and, so far, that's one of the aircraft which guests *don't* get to go prowling around inside...

A few *Fencers* have been exported, but not many, and not the fully capable versions, either. Libya and Syria, along with a few other nations, have been sold the Su-24MK. It seems that the Russians don't want significant numbers of *Fencers* going to other countries (except, perhaps, at low level, at high speed, and with an attitude).

(Below) As soon as their boots hit the concrete after returning from a mission these *Fencer* pilots lit up cigarettes and started an intensive debriefing session, before some even bothered to remove their helmets. There was nothing casual about these discussions, and a roving photographer was simply ignored. Note ground crew working on the braking chute stowage in the background.

Fencer tails; the unit at Kubinka display both this light gray scheme with white details, and conventional brown/green camouflage. The former may possibly be a special exercise identification scheme.

Su-24 crews show off a variety of flight jackets (we particularly liked the beat-up two-tone brown hide model), harness, "speed jeans" worn over a camouflage suit, and dark blue "off season" flight clothing. The helmet is the ZSh-1M, with the comfortably lined KM-32 oxygen mask.

(Right) Fencer pilot and crew chief debrief after a training mission; the former wears the winter flight suit and the newer helmet, the latter the ShZ-61 communications helmet – also often seen worn by helicopter crews, and by jet pilots underneath older "bone domes" such as the ZSh-3 which lack integral communications.

Fencer fin with braking parachute stowage; as soon as the aircraft returns to the blocks after landing the chute is cut away and a new one fitted.

(Right) It is rare to be allowed to photograph a powered-up cockpit. This is the "office" of the Su-24, with side-by-side Severin K-36D ejector seats for the pilot at left and the WSO, or "*shturman*", at right. The instrument in the centre of the panel is the radar attack warning display, indicating the relative bearing of the threat. Here safety cables are clipped to the ejection handles.

(Below and right) *Fencer* pilot, ejector seat and split canopy details. The individualistic bourgeois practice of embellishing flight helmets is not as popular in Russia as in the West, but it's catching on; from his decal this pilot seems to be claiming sponsorship by Esso!

Su-25 "Frogfoot"

Squadron commander Lt.Col. Valery Kravtsov taxying out a Sukhoi Su-25UB, the trainer model of the *Frogfoot* close air support ship, with a young lieutenant in the front seat for a check ride, and pairs of gas tanks and rocket pods on the inboard wing pylons. Unlike the USAF's A-10, the Su-25 (known in Russian as *grach*, "rook", but more popularly to its crews as *cheburashka*, "little critter") can use short dirt strips near the forward edge of battle area, even with a full load of ordnance on that seemingly endless row of pylons – almost 10,000 pounds of bombs, rockets and missiles.

Lt.Col.Kravstov and his student are latched into the Su-25UB, and start working through the checklist; note the hood behind the front-seater, used during instrument training. Apart from his usual command duties Valery Kravtsov is the leader of the Su-25 aerobatic team, the Sky Hussars, and he likes to wring out this amazingly taut, agile little airplane at low level over the field.

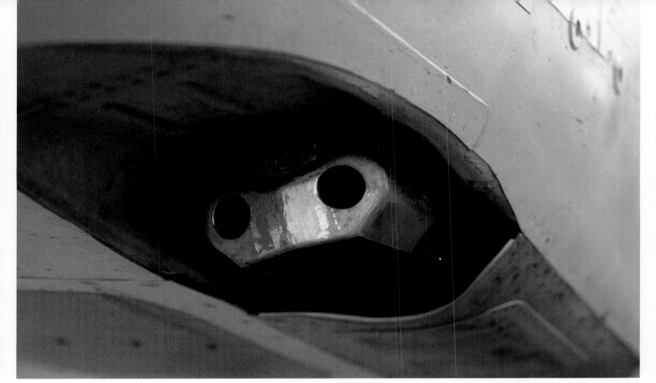

(Left) Final checks by the crew chief, here fondling the nose sensors. The Su-25K used in Afghanistan had the *Klon* laser rangefinder; the most recent model Su-25T, a "stretched" single-seater based on this trainer version, has a much more sophisticated *Voshod* navigation/attack package. At bottom right note the muzzles of the twin 30mm cannon.

(Above) Close-up of the AO-17A port nose mounting of the twin 30mm cannon. When they open up a massive fireball lights up the port side of the aircraft.

These big rounds weigh some two pounds each, with projectiles over an inch in diameter.

A single-seat Su-25K, as clean as this airframe ever gets, leaves the runway. Since it is designed to work low and slow, the top speed of around Mach .7 is quite adequate. In Afghanistan from 1982, this most effective of Russian close support jets worked to perfect joint tactics with the Mi-24 *Hind* attack helicopters. Just visible is the differently configured outermost pylon of the five under each wing; this mounts the AA-8 *Aphid* self-defense missile. Afghan combat experience led to various modifications from around 1988, including integral flare dispensers in the tail and above the engine tailpipes, the latter flanked by an airscoop to bleed cooling air into the exhaust wash; internal armor was fitted to prevent fire spreading from one engine to the other. About 300 of these muscular little jets are in Russian service, and others fly with a few foreign air forces.

(Left) Su-25K cockpit, powered up, though with the ejector seat safety cables still in place.

A pair of "little critters" – an Su-25K and an Su-25UB armed trainer – make a formation take-off past the big tracking radar vans in the middle of the airfield.

The Su-25 will fly happily on either avgas or diesel – in fact, on virtually anything but pure vodka.

(Below) 57mm free-flight rocket pods as mounted on the Su-25.

Su-27 "Flanker"

Capt. Sergey Samko is one of the lucky pilots who not only get to fly the big Su-27, but have also been selected for a posting to Kubinka, within reach of the relative fleshpots of Moscow. Like many other *Flanker* pilots at the base he is a volunteer demonstration pilot in addition to his regular tactical training activities.

It is entirely arguable that the best air-to-air combat fighter in service in the world today is the Sukhoi Su-27, a big, fast, extremely agile airplane that is at least the equal of the Western air superiority fighters it was designed to challenge.

Its principal missions are bomber escort and interception, and with ten missile stations and a 30mm cannon the *Flanker* is a threat to any airplane within its engagement range. Until recently it shared the air superiority fighter role with the MiG-29, but the Sukhoi's better range and performance have now made it the sole contender for the job.

Like other modern multi-role fighters the *Flanker* is designed to fight three kinds of battles: long range ("beyond visual range", BVR), intermediate, and close range. Its pulse-Doppler look-down, shoot-down radar has a published maximum range of about 150 miles and a track-while-scan capability. Maximum speed is Mach 2.35 – a fairly meaningless figure since it is seldom employed; more important is the aircraft's agility and acceleration, both of which are extremely high. For a fighter that is as big as a World War II medium bomber the Su-27 squirms and dashes very well, making it a good gunfighter as well as a world-class missile platform.

The *Flanker* will get airborne from rugged dirt strips and roads, if necessary, with a reasonable combat load, in a couple of thousand feet. From a good long runway the Su-27 can burn into the sky at a take-off weight of over 66,000 pounds. With internal fuel alone its combat radius is about 930 miles; with aerial refueling you can fly the thing across all eight time zones from Moscow to Vladivostok, but even at Mach 2 you will have a sore butt when you get there. Ceiling is rated at 59,000ft., and it can get there faster than any other combat aircraft in its class – or any other class, either. The Su-27 has snatched about 30 world records for aircraft performance, many from the F-15 Eagle that it was designed to fight.

The *Flanker* is a seriously big fighter – 48 feet across the wing tips, 71 feet long, almost 20 feet to the top of the fin. Its construction is quite conventional, without any of the composites used in the MiG-29 or F-15E. The entire airframe uses a smooth, blended design approach which Sukhoi calls an "integrated" airframe, producing lift as one very large airfoil. It generally resembles both the F-15 and MiG-29, with twin fins, underslung engines and lots of other features shared by many modern fighters. They were all designed to do essentially the same thing, and the specifications and the wind tunnels demand the same solution to a problem no matter who is working on it.

The huge wing seems as big as a tennis court. The leading edge blends smoothly into the fuselage, all the way up to the radome, generating lift all the way. Leading edge flaps provide extra lift for take-

off and landing. Instead of conventional ailerons and flaps the Sukhoi wing uses "flaperons" that combine both functions, both in combat manoeuvers (under full computer control) and during routine landing and take-off.

Like most of its contemporaries (though not the MiG-29), the Su-27 uses an inherently unstable design coupled with an SDU-27 computer-driven ("fly by wire") flight control system to retain agility. The four-channel flight control computer incorporates a stability augmentation system (SAS). The SAS technology takes a great deal of the work out of fly-

A UB-model Su-27 taxying out to the active runway for an air combat practice mission in the Kubinka training area. These photos show how very little actual similarity there is between the Sukhoi and the F-15 Eagle with which it was generally compared a few years ago. One difference pictures can't convey is the fact that these guys launch *fast*: they start engines and get airborne in less time than it takes the average F-15 pilot to do his preflight, and taxy speeds seem about twice as fast as on American bases.

About 1,100 feet down the runway from brake release, accelerating through about 135 knots, with first notch of flaps and in burner, this big *Flanker* is headed for the clouds. Although the Su-27 has FOD protection doors for the engine air intakes they use a screen design rather than the solid slabs seen on the MiG-29.

ing any aircraft, and they are found in most modern high-performance combat types, both fixed- and rotary-wing. Even so, the flight controls are generally set rather more stiff than in Western combat aircraft; the pilot of the Su-27 sets the amount of resistance to suit himself.

It is a single-seat fighter, and at the "man/machine interface" to which your butt gets strapped the author can report that it is a hard seat, too. Early versions of the aircraft – the ones shown in this book – use what Roy Braybrook calls "steam gauge" instrumentation, but recent production models use cathode ray tube (CRT) "glass cockpit" technologies similar to Western fighters like the F/A-18 Hornet and F-15E Strike Eagle. The Russians have been quite candid about their cockpits; Professor Samolovich (see below) told me that "...our electronics are much inferior to yours in terms of size, weight, and reliability." You will notice, however, that he didn't say anything about capability.

One of the virtues of Russian aircraft design is the standardization of cockpit layout from one type to another. You can climb out of a MiG-21 or -29 and into a *Foxbat* or *Flanker* and know where everything is without having to get out a diagram from the "dash one." That doesn't mean that they all use the same instruments; but standardization is part of the design process that helps a pilot manage the aircraft during times of high workload. It makes transition faster and easier, and it partially reduces the problems of a "head down" cockpit. Even so, the newest Flankers are getting HOTAS ("hands on throttle and stick") technologies, along with CRTs.

One of the fascinating surprises of my visit to Russia came from an interview with one of the most senior and respected men in the aviation industry, Professor Oleg Samolovich. I had always heard how slow and bureaucratic Soviet aircraft design was; but Professor Samolovich told me that the basic design of the *Flanker* was accomplished in three days – by

A two-seat Su-27UB makes a low pass before entering the "cobra" manoeuver. Unlike the MiG-29UB the Su-27 trainer is a fully functional combat aircraft with complete radar and weapons systems. The Sukhoi has been selected as Russia's standard fighter for the future, which probably has a bearing on the development of a naval version, and the emphasis on introducing modern "glass cockpit" technologies for this type.

If anybody else tried this, in any other airplane, they would promptly die... 80 knots airspeed, angle of attack around 80 degrees, about 300 feet above the unforgiving earth: the big *Flanker* demonstrates the incredible "cobra" deceleration manoeuver, and lives to tell the tale. The slight glow from the tailpipe reveals that the burner has been lit, and the aircraft will soon start to fly conventionally again, nose first. The "cobra" amazed the Paris air show audience, not least by its conclusive demonstration that Russian engines, long sneered at by the ignorant, were reliable and responsive under conditions that Western pilots dared not duplicate.

himself and two others, one of whom was a graduate student! That was in 1969, and of course it took years of effort on the part of thousands of men and women to bring the preliminary design to maturity; the prototype finally flew for the first time in May 1977.

That first version was designated the T-10, and its development program was plagued with crashes and delays. One of the prototypes was stripped of all extra weight – including paint – and used to challenge numerous performance records between 1986 and 1988. That aircraft, designated P-42, captured 27 records, many from a similarly stripped-down version of the F-15 (the "Streak Eagle").

One of the reasons for the *Flanker's* record-breaking performance is Russian superiority in the understanding and application of aerodynamics. It is one of the areas where, despite the availability of the very large scale computers used by Western developers, the Soviet aircraft designers had a clear edge over American and European manufacturers. Part of that superiority is the result of a close partnership between all of the design bureaux (OKBs) and the Russian equivalent of NASA, the Central Aerodynamics Institute research bureau (called TsAGI).

(Left and below left) *Flankers* of the Russian Knights display team show off their paces and, as one swings hard to port before popping his gear and air-brake, their gaudy color scheme.

(Below) A pair of Su-27s in tight formation with a Tupolev Tu-160 *Blackjack* strategic bomber. The first Russian design to dispense with defensive cannon, the swing-wing Tu-160 has a combat radius of about 4,500 miles on internal fuel, Mach 2.3 maximum speed, and is designed to launch cruise or attack missiles or free-fall bombs.

Short final, gear down and locked, spoiler and flaps out, power back: a *Flanker* from the Russian Knights slides over the numbers back to Kubinka's chilly concrete.

This *Flanker* pilot is 6ft.2in. tall, but fits reasonably comfortably into the Sukhoi's big cockpit. Note the HUD, smaller than the huge display system of the F-15E but quite advanced by any standards; and, ahead of the windshield, the "eye" of the impressive passive infrared tracker and laser rangefinder systems.

It's the same the world over: the pilots go out and have their fun, get the airplane dirty and probably bend something, then give it back to the ground crew – "Hey, you guys get this thing fixed; I'm going to the club for a beer"...

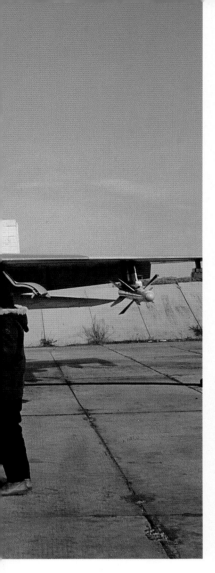

(Above and left) *Flanker* pilot Valery Romanov, serving on an air defense base at Komsomolsk on the Amur River in Russia's far east, clambers up and straps in; he wears a high visibility full pressure G-suit and the ZSh-1M helmet. This specifically designed ladder is part of the *Flanker's* standard ground equipment; there is even a small brush built into the bottom rung to clean the mud off your boots.

This is a logical point to salute my colleague Sergey Skrynnikov, a Sukhoi staff photographer who spends a lot of time riding around in Russian aircraft. He's even dropped in on the carrier *Kiev* to take some of the first shots of Russian deck trials. The only aircraft Sergey refuses to fly in is the Yak-38 *Forger*, the early VTOL design which first gave the Soviets a limited naval fighter capability, but which has a troubled history. That's because – unlike the British designed Harrier, with its vectored-thrust engine – the Yak depends on two lift engines for take-off thrust; and a problem with either one of them is apt to be terminal. *(Sergey Skrynnikov/ AviaData via Arms Communications)*

Detail of Su-27 tail section. A pair of cruciform braking parachutes are available inside the tail cone, although the huge dorsal air brake is usually all it takes to decelerate the *Flanker* on landing.

(Left and right) Two angles on the Su-27 cockpit. Although Russian cockpits have been criticized for their clutter and complexity, their layout is highly standardized. This makes transition training much simpler, since the pilot knows, without thinking, where most of the secondary controls and instruments are. Note the red handles for the Severin K-36D ejector seat (an excellent piece of equipment, though cruelly hard on the posterior...) The handles are "safed" by rotation to this configuration, and "armed" by rotating them 90 degrees so that the two segments lie parallel to the pilot's thighs. This is simpler than arming the equivalent Western seats, which require the removal of several security pins.

Su-27 control column detail. Besides the normal controls for radar "squawk", missile management, trim, and weapons launch (trigger in front, not visible here), an auto-recovery feature ("panic switch") will extract the aircraft from almost any ham-fisted manoeuver a pilot can get himself into.

(Right) The *Flanker's* stern aspect is a shape unique among modern combat aircraft. Note in this view the flare and chaff dispensers – the rows of holes flanking each side of the tail cone. The entire horizontal tail surfaces move under command of the four-channel flight control computer.

(Below) An "alert bird", with functional missiles, on stand-by at Komsomolsk in the Russian far east. *(Sergey Skrynnikov/ AviaData via Arms Communications)*

The scale of the Su-27's tailpipe is indicated in this pose by six-footer Maj.Alexander Datalov, who serves with a tactical squadron and is also a volunteer with the Red Knights *Flanker* display team. Datalov is the kind of friendly, intense, energetic, professional pilot you find in the squadrons of air forces around the world, with an ego that would not fit in a barn – based on a career of exemplary performance. Perhaps some day the major and his squadron mates will get a chance to train with their NATO contemporaries, a real "red on blue" training scenario without the bloodshed. It will be interesting to see who would have won the air combat segment of World War III...

(Below) The fireball from the GSh-301 30mm cannon is huge, and to protect the airframe from erosion the area around the muzzle is a titanium fairing. Barrel life is short – the bore wears out after around 2,000 rounds – but the system is extremely accurate.

Photo opportunities of American "war shot" missiles (as opposed to drill rounds) are rare; but the Russians genially offered to trot out this rack of AA-11 *Archers* from a ready ammunition storage bunker near the flight line.

The ground crew mount an *Archer* much as an American crew would a Sidewinder; lug spacing on the pylons is supposed to be the same, at 14ins., as on NATO aircraft. These armorers are attaching the electrical umbilical to the connection on the front of the launch rail. Only when the missile is secured will they remove the red protective covers for the seeker head and fins.

The *Archer,* which bears the Russian designation R-73, uses thrust vectoring plus aerodynamic controls to achieve the kind of high-G agility required to defeat aerial targets in close combat. This nozzle shot shows the four control vanes.

(Above and below) The weapon is installed, and the protective covers removed, although the red safety clip is still in place. This is a genuine "war shot", not a practice missile. Not a lot is known in the West about the details of its performance; but knowledgeable observers speculate that the AA-11, with a new seeker comparable to that on late-model Sidewinders, has significant advantages in terms of launch angles and manoeuvrability, and may be the most potent short-range IR homing missile in the world.

For the purposes of these captions we will refer to the navalized *Flanker* as Su-27K (for *korabelny*, "naval"). This shot shows the canards peculiar to this model.

So far Russian carriers lack steam catapults, but use the same arrestor wire system as Western carriers. This close-up shows the Su-27K's arrestor hook.

Over the bleak landscape of the Russian far east, a navalized Su-27K up from Komsomolsk base turns hard to port, displaying inert training missiles – long-range AA-10 *Alamos* on the centerline stations, and short-range AA-11 *Archers* at the wingtips. *(Sergey Skrynnikov/AviaData via Arms Communications)*

The navalized version of the *Flanker*, intended for the new full-deck carriers of the *Admiral Kuznetsov* class, has been referred to by several different designations according to source, including Su-27KU and Su-27IB. The knowledgeable Jon Lake of *World Air Power Journal* believes that the OKB designation may be T-10-42. It has a retractable refueling probe on the port side of the nose ahead of the cockpit; this shot shows one tanking at fairly low level during a flight over the Zhukovskiy test center. *(Sergey Skrynnikov/AviaData via Arms Communications)*

An Su-27K photographed at Kubinka, showing the folding wings of this version; the weapons (black bands identifying them as display rounds only) are a pair of heat-seeking AA-11 *Archers* and an AA-10c *Alamo* extended range semi-active radar guided missile.
(Yefim Gordon/AviaData via Arms Communications)

Pilot and gunner of an Mi-24P *Hind* attack helicopter chat before a training mission; quite a number of Russian aircrew of types flying low-level missions wear camouflaged suits as part of their flight wardrobe.

Ground Attack: Mi-24 "Hind"

The Mi-24 attack helicopter, NATO codename *Hind*, is yet another example of interesting Russian aircraft design. The *Hind D*, the most common variant (and for once matching the Russian designation, Mi-24D) is essentially a helicopter gunship with a secondary role as an armed transport, but there are at least nine major variants of the basic design in service with numerous countries. It has been through several important versions since it was introduced about 25 years ago, and the current version looks little like the first *Hind*, confusingly designated the B-model by NATO. Like America's "Huey" the Mi-24 evolved into a multi-role aircraft, with attack, gunship, helicopter escort, and assault troop carrying missions. Eight troops can be carried, or four litter patients. The *Hind* story differs from that of the Huey, however, in that the attack and gunship role was built in, not added on; and it seems to fit better.

About 2,500 total airframes have been delivered to the Soviet Army, and many more to Cuba, Libya, Poland, South Yemen, North Korea, and other nations. An export version, a down-rated model of the standard gunship, is the Mi-25. The export anti-armor *Hind* is confusingly identified as the Mi-35.

Power is furnished by a pair of Isotov TV3-117 turboshaft gas turbines, each delivering up to 2,200 shaft horsepower. Maximum take-off weight for the D-model is 26,500 pounds, although the figure for normal missions will be about 2,000 pounds lighter; that includes up to 3,300 pounds of ordnance, or eight combat troops, but not both. Cruise speed is 145 knots, with VNE rated at 181 knots. Ceiling (out of ground effect) is about 14,000 feet. The heli-

(Right) In Russia kids pay as much attention to "Do Not Touch the Exhibits" signs as kids the world over. This museum piece, included here for contrast, is the forefather of the *Hind* series, the Mi-24A, confusingly codenamed *Hind B* by NATO. It had side-by-side seating, and a 12.7mm machine gun in a chin turret controlled by a gunner in the nose ahead of the pilot and co-pilot.

Hind **pilot portrait; note that he wears the same ZSh-1M bone dome as jet pilots.**

Ми-24В

ВЕРТОЛЕТ ОГНЕВОЙ ПОДДЕРЖКИ
ОКБ им МИЛЯ М.Л. 1979)
ДЛИНА ФЮЗЕЛЯЖА, М
ДИАМЕТР НЕСУЩЕГО ВИНТА
ВЗЛЕТНЫЙ ВЕС, КГ   12 000
СКОРОСТЬ МАКС.,КМ/Ч   335
ПОТОЛОК, М   4 500
ДАЛЬНОСТЬ ПОЛЕТА,КМ   1 050
ВООРУЖЕНИЕ: НУРС, АВИАБОМБЫ
ПУЛЕМЕТ КАЛИБРА 127 ММ
ПТУРС

copter can climb out at about 2,500 feet per minute – but not with a full load on the weapons stations and a full bag of gas. Depending on load, the combat radius for the D-model Hind is from 100 to about 180 miles. Maximum endurance is rated at four hours, but that is a long time to sit in any helicopter.

The fuselage of the model NATO calls the *Hind D* is not quite 60 feet long, with the pilot and gunner seated in individual tandem cockpits behind an armored skin about a quarter-inch thick; a flight engineer's station is in the main troop compartment aft. (The earliest Mi-24 – NATO designation *Hind-B* – was configured with a side-by-side cockpit, which was soon changed.) Titanium is used extensively in the aircraft for strength and weight reduction. The armored panels that surround the cockpits are large, smooth sheets devoid of any visible fasteners. Critical flight components are all armored, particularly the engines and drive train. The pilot and gunner's positions are separate, armored stations with redundant flight controls and weapons systems to allow either crew member to perform essential duties in an emergency. Both have armored glass windscreens for protection against small arms fire. Accomodations are fairly spacious, for a gunship. The pilot, in the aft station, is well above the gunner and looks over his head. The gunner has several sighting systems to contend with.

Drooping winglets with six stations for external stores provide the *Hind* with tremendous offensive

firepower potential. All sorts of weapons can be installed: missiles, rocket pods, cannon, mine dispensers, and chemical weapon dispensers. These winglets are about 22 feet tip-to-tip, and are estimated to provide about 25 percent of the helicopter's lift in level cruise flight. A gunsight camera is installed in the outboard portion of the left winglet.

The D-model was typically shipped with a YakB-12.7 rotary four-barrel 12.7mm (.50cal) machine gun in a powered chin turret slaved to the gunner's sight. During the Afghan War, when the *mujahideen* themselves acquired 12.7mm weapons and proved that the *Hind* was not always as invulnerable as its reputation suggested, a new gunship appeared. This Mi-24P (*Hind F*) variant, illustrated in our photos, has a GSh-30-2 long-range twin-barrel 30mm cannon in fixed mounts on the starboard side of the nose, with a forward-looking infrared/low-light television sensor sighting system.

Although currently a bit out of date in the anti-armor role, particularly when compared to the Mi-28 *Havoc*, Ka-50 *Hokum* and the US Apache, the Mi-24 is still an important element in the battle plans of commanders who own them. The helicopter normally carries four AT-6 anti-armor missiles, two on each outboard winglet station, along with four rocket canisters and the 30mm cannon. The *Hind E* model is a dedicated anti-armor weapon designed specifically for tank busting; this version carries up to 12 AT-6s, and is equipped with a radar guidance system.

Compare the old Mi-24A with this latest Mi-24P, all wound up to hover-taxy to the pad and await departure clearance from the tower. Encrusted with warts, tusks and barnacles, there can surely be few more menacing-looking attack aircraft than a late-model *Hind*.

(Below) The men of a helicopter demonstration team that participates in air shows all over Russia; they are a great bunch of guys, and they make their Mi-24s do things which you later wonder if you could *really* have seen the way you remember them...

Despite the large size of the Mi-24, the demonstration team wrings the helicopters out with a very impressive flying display – on this occasion, in and out of snow flurries.

(Right) Both pilot (aft) and gunner are well protected by titanium armor and bullet-resistant windscreens. Their canopies are still just plexiglass, but even so they enjoy more protection – and a lot more firepower – than most US helo crews in Vietnam ever got. At bottom right, with its armor doors closed, is the pod accomodating the infrared/low-light TV sensor sights and the command guidance antenna for the AT-6 *Spiral* anti-tank missile sometimes carried by the *Hind*.

Starboard side detail of the Mi-24P. Note the dome-shaped "hot brick" system mounted behind the rotor, to jam heat-seeking missiles, and behind the red star the ASO-3 flare dispensers; Afghanistan was a harsh school.

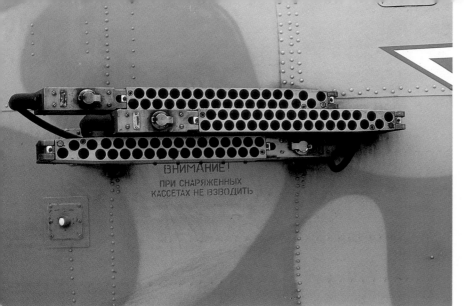

Detail of the ASO-3 flare dispenser racks.

(Right) The long GSh-30-2 30mm cannon mounted on the starboard nose are the distinguishing feature of the Mi-24P; combat experience in Afghanistan led to this replacement for the YakB four-barrel rotary 12.7mm machine gun chin turret of the *Hind D.* The armored fairing below housing the FLIR/TV system has protective doors controlled from the gunner's cockpit.

(Left and above) Mi-24P Hind gunner's cockpit detail – basic flight controls and instruments are duplicated here; and the view forward from the gunner's seat.

353243202751Z

ВНИМАНИЕ!
9М114 ДОСЫЛАТЬ
РУКОЯТКОЙ ПЛАВН

The drooping winglets of the Mi-24P provide a tremendous amount of supplementary lift, as well as stowage for a lot of ordnance. The 57mm free flight rocket pod is standard; the new rails at the wingtips are for the tube-launched AT-6 *Spiral*.

(Below) A protoype of the single-seat Kamov Ka-50 *Hokum* – Russian name "Werewolf" – which won the Soviet Army's competition for a new generation attack helicopter against the Mi-28. Among its advanced features is an ejector seat, which operates after the rotors have been blown away. The bulge under the early- configuration nose houses the stabilized laser guidance system for "Whirlwind" long-range anti-armor missiles. On the starboard side is the housing for a hydraulically controlled 24A2 30mm cannon, which can be depressed and has limited traverse. The winglets have pylons for a variety of free-flight and guided ordnance. *(Sergey Skrynnikov/AviaData via Arms Communications)*

Cockpit of the Mi-28 *Havoc*; armed with a 30mm chin-mounted 24A2 cannon, 40 x 80mm free-flight rockets and 16 anti-armor guided missiles, this potent attack helicopter has many advanced features including Doppler radar for navigation and low light sensors. One rumoured version that had a lot of my friends in US Army AH-64 Apache units looking thoughtful was a model configured as a dedicated air-to-air fighter – nowadays they are just worried that they won't find a way to get a ride in it.*(Sergey Skrynnikov/ AviaData via Arms Communications)*
